By
Ryusho Jeffus

Ten Suchnesses: Equality Despite Their Differences
Volume II Ichinen Sanzen

Ten Suchnesses
· By Ryusho Jeffus
Copyright 2018

Myosho-ji, Wonderful Voice Buddhist Temple
611 Vine St.
Syracuse, NY 13203

ISBN-13: 978-1726325523
ISBN-10: 1726325520

Contents

Introduction

Lately my time has been greatly occupied with printmaking, that is carving blocks from which I then make prints. The process requires multiple skills. First an image needs to be made. Once the image has been put on the block then all of the areas that are not to be printed are carved away using special knives. This can be a rather lengthy and tedious process depending upon the complexity of the design. Once the block is carved it is inked up and then an impression made from the inked block. For the images in this book I also hand made the paper they were printed on.

The images for this book were all drawn directly upon the block and from my mind. I had some general concepts I wanted to illustrate but in an abstract way. My intent was to make images that could mean any number of things to various people. I didn't want things to be so concrete as to leave the viewer out of the process of discovery.

Once I had finished with most of the blocks, eight to be exact, I felt ready to write the book for them. Because there is not much written about the Ten Aspects or Ten Suchnesses I thought it might be useful for a book to be written to explain them a bit so people can have a better idea of the depth and complexity of not just the Ten Suchnesses but also the concept of Ichinen Sanzen, Three

Thousands States of Mind in a Moments Existence, a fundamental teaching of the Lotus Sutra as identified by Chih'I or Tientai.

As you read this book you will see that it is less a direct exposition on the meaning of each of the Ten Factors and more of journey through their interconnectedness and interdependence. Unlike the Ten Worlds which can easily be described independently, the Ten Factors are deeply connected and intertwined in such a way that extracting them out from the group deprives them of the mutual affect they have on each other. In fact one of the Factors is the mutuality of all ten, the equality of each despite their differences.

That they are each different is true, yet they are so intertwined that the equality is a crucial aspect. Their mutuality and equality means that fundamentally there is not one without the other nine. I hope that through the course of this book you can follow this thought.

Ten Aspects

Briefly and perhaps harmfully The Ten Aspects are as follows:

Appearance - Briefly, this is the way you look. This is not fixed as you can smile and appear one way or scowl and appear another. You can wear certain clothes and look different from when you wear other types of clothing. There are some aspects of appearance which are not changeable such as eye color, or skin color (well not so much generally), height once fully grown, hair color (well not permanently for the most part), hair or no hair. I would add gender except in certain circumstances.

Nature - This is how you are, not who you are. This includes such things as pessimistic, optimistic, daring, bold, shy, extrovert, introvert, gregarious, quick learner, visual learner, literal learner, learner by doing rather than instruction, adventurous, laid back, easy going, excitable. These are not always fixed, though for some people they may seem to be such. And further they are not always the same in any of us, we can be one way at one time and another in other instances. We can be both shy and gregarious, introverted and extroverted.

Entity - This is our total complete self, it can include genetics, disposition to certain diseases, blood type, physical strength, emotional strength, internal organs, demeanor as a total picture,

Power - Is not always only about physical or mental strength. It includes our ability to persevere, to challenge ourselves, to introspect, to reflect, (our nature may affect our willingness or tendency to do so even if we may have great power as an ability). Our ability to lead others, for good or ill, our skill with other people can be a power again for good or ill. Our ability to see our strengths and use them skillfully or not is a power even when the actual power may be limited. A person may not have the power to do something yet may be able to accomplish the goal through the power of working with others again for good or for ill.

Activity - What are we doing, what are we accomplishing or trying to accomplish, is the activity physical, mental, emotional, spiritual, is the activity for self or for others are some ways to consider activity.

Primary Cause - There is a cause which precedes every cause to some extent. There is a primary cause in all things, what is that in each of the situations we engage in and how does that impact all the other Ten Aspects. One primary cause is the difference between self and others, between self and environment, between self as a physical entity and self as a spiritual entity and self as a complete undifferentiated complete entity. Where is the primary cause directed inward versus outward, towards oneself or towards others, includes or excludes others, benefits others or only self all are primary causes beneath initial traditional activities. Also a primary cause is human, non-human animal, plant, or even alien.

Environmental Cause - There are factors which take place outside ourselves and often outside our control. Is it raining, if so did you think to bring an umbrella? Failing to consider environmental causes can lead to death such as by heat exhaustion and stroke, or freezing to death, starvation, disease and illness. Sometimes the environment is beyond our control but what is within our control may be able to mitigate the effects of the environment. Sometimes it can not, such as an earthquake, typhoon, airplane crash, fire, terrorist attack. In all cases we do ever act independent of our environment even if we may fail to consider it.

Effect - It's what happens, seen, unseen, known, unknown, immediately observable or seemingly manifest later (all effects manifest instantly only some may not be observed instantly)

Reward or Negative reward (retribution) - Sometimes what seems to be boon may be an albatross. What is negative now may end up being reward to our future growth and development. These are not absolutes except in how we treat them. Could motivate us into changing poison into medicine

Equality - there is complete equality and connectedness throughout these aspects which is one of the aspects. A subtle change in on causes a ripple throughout all. This is why it is important to not try to completely separate these as we try to understand them in our lives. No one aspect can be truly removed or analyzed independent of the others. This is their equality despite their differences.

Appearance: Nyoze So

My mother had a habitual facial expression which clearly
showed when she was less than pleased with something.
She perfected the art of the pursed-lip-exasperation-hiss
and used it liberally throughout her life. As she got older
and suffered more from the effects of Chronic Obstructive
Pulmonary Disease, COPD, the pursing of lips and the
exaggerated his became more pronounced. In fact for
patients suffering the effects of COPD there is a breathing
technique called pursed-lip-breathing. You can try this
little exercise on yourself quite easily to see how beneficial
it can be.

First exhale only through your nose. Try to get as much
air out of your lungs as you can. It's important in this
experiment to keep your lips firmly closed and to only
breath out through your nose. Remember this is just a
little experiment. Now without inhaling purse your lips
and push out more air. With your lips closed you can't get
as much air out of your lungs as you can with your lips
slightly parted.

A common misunderstanding about some COPD related
conditions is that is not about inhaling, or getting
oxygenated air. Part of the misunderstanding is because
we see COPD patients with oxygen tanks and tubes to their
noses. What's really going on is COPD patients are less

able to flex their lungs to fully exhale the carbon dioxide from their lungs. The oxygen is to increase the amount of oxygenated air they inhale thereby offsetting the large volume of CO2 that remains in the lungs on the exhale.

So COPD patients use pursed-lip breathing for survival.

Now, my mother had that habitual facial expression of displeasure that is now enhanced because of her need to purse her lips to offset the effects of COPD. This meant that she almost always seemed to be scowling and displeased, and mostly she was. Her facial expression of displeasure was a constant feature and so at times it was difficult relating to her not knowing if she was or was not actually displeased.

Her appearance affected how everyone who encountered her reacted to her. I'm not a therapist and if I was I would not be qualified to analyze her because I was her son and would be too emotionally involved. Yet I do wonder if her unhappiness in her last years of life was self generated or if it was a reaction to how other people reacted to her appearance of constant displeasure at things. Most likely it was a lot of both. My mother was a deeply unhappy person most of her later years.

Anyway, I don't want this to be about my mother rather about how our appearance affects others which in turn has ramifications in every aspect of our lives. You only need to ask a black person about how shop keeper react when they enter a store and how that makes them feel. I know that in my own early adulthood I would also be followed around stores, probably because of all my tattoos. It almost made me feel like steeling something since I was tried and convicted of theft just by being me.

I can only inadequately begin to imagine how difficult it is for a black person to experience that their entire lives. They live lives and navigate in a society that has already accused them of multiple crimes for which they never committed. Think of the high rate of murders of black people by law enforcement.

Our appearance has a significant affect on the shape of our lives, the way we process, the way we interact, the options available to us, the doors opened or closed, the opportunities given or withheld and so on.

Appearance also includes the clothes we wear, the style of our hair, the tattoos on our body, the piercings we have, the nail polish, the shoes, the tie, the everything. Fair it may not be, yet it is a fact. Yes attitudes change and that is often a good thing, and as the attitudes change so does the effect of various appearance items. Now tattoos are more generally accepted in public but now I'm old and so I get a different response from people and it isn't always pleasant, lol.

So, our appearance which includes things we can not change as well as things we can, is part of the Ten Aspects and an important part of what happens, what we experience, what we live on a moment by moment basis.

Self No Self

When I was in my final training to be a chaplain one of the supervisors of our unit would occasionally make a point of showing his ignorance of Buddhism by miss-quoting and miss-interpreting a common cliché expression of no-self. He would say things like "I thought you were supposed to be no-self" or such. Which in my mind is absurd and as I mentioned a misrepresentation, a convenient ignorance for him to hide behind.

The thing is, it is not no-self, it really is neither self nor no-self. In other words it is the space between self and no-self. I like to say that we as Buddhist wallow in the spaces in between, we romp in the grey areas.

So what exactly does this mean for us in our practice. Well here's the way I see it. In the Four Lower Worlds of Hell, Hunger, Animality, Anger the primary focus of an individual is towards one's self. There is suffering and the desire to eliminate the suffering however because self is the focus of those in the lower worlds the self misdiagnoses the causes and the solutions.

The greatest value of the Ten Worlds is its function as a GPS to navigate out of suffering. The quickest way is to approach the World of Humanity. And the most prominent characteristic of Humanity is thinking of others. It is the beginning of empathy, sympathy, connection, compassion, communication and it has space of the consideration of others.

So, humanity then becomes less self and more no-self in that it begins to turn the self towards others. The Buddha, when he first began his austerities after sampling all the various teachers available during his time, approached the goal of enlightenment as the total obliteration of self. By annihilating the self the Buddha thought it would allow enlightenment, yet what he discovered is that it quickly leads to death.

When he was completely emaciated and could hardly support his own skeleton, nearly falling in a lake and drowning he realized that these austerities were not the path to eliminating suffering and would not allow him to fulfill his goal of finding a path to teach others how to end their suffering.

Taking a bowl of gruel nourishment and sitting under the Bodhi tree the Buddha meditated and realized it is the middle path that leads to enlightenment and is a path which all humans are able to travel.

For us it begins with a little less self. Slowly as our life begins to change and we create space for the consideration of others we focus less on our self and more on others. As this increases we have more space for others and find that we need less space for self.

So it is neither self nor no-self it is the space between that has a self-others direction.

At first when we are moving into Humanity from the Four Lower Worlds it isn't necessary to have great compassion or great empathy. It is enough to realize that others too are suffering and that there are solutions that lift not only self out of suffering but also provides a way for others.

Think of the banquet in the realm of Hunger. Each diner is seated in front of the most scrumptious meal imaginable, however the utensils are six feet long. As long as each person focuses on self they don't get to eat. However, when we turn our attention outwards we can see that it is possible to feed each other, say for example across the table. Thereby everyone gets to eat and everyone ends their hunger.

It doesn't take much, just a little bit less self and a little bit more others and life begins to change and the change keeps expanding as the skill and space is made to consider less self and more others.

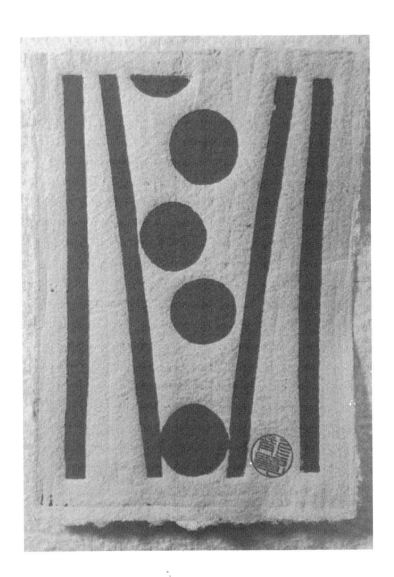

Selecting/Sorting Criteria: Nyoze Tai

Do you tend to be what you would consider a rational deliberative processor? Or would you consider yourself to be more spur of the moment or rash in your decisions? Perhaps some of both at different times. And further what skills do you bring to those moments of decision?

Sometimes people make decisions with out the proper understanding of the situation or consequences or even because there were no other options.

Years ago when I worked for Bank of America I used to volunteer one night a week at the headquarters of Goodwill in Charlotte teaching financial literacy classes. Sometimes the students were people who may be recovering from homelessness, or perhaps release from incarceration, or even new immigrants to the US.

Each group of people showed up with unique perspectives towards money, spending, and saving. And those unique perspectives caused them to act upon their circumstances in different ways. It was not possible to teach the same material, as it continually had to be adjusted to the mindset of the students. It was quite fascinating, educational, and might I be selfish enough to say rewarding.

Let's look at immigrants, especially those from societies based upon cash only. These are places where credit is not heard of and does not enter the mindset of the people or culture. In fact credit is frequently abhorred and avoided at all costs if even at all. Here they are in the US which generally avoids cash or has greatly reduced the circulation of currency. To some from other countries even a debit card has a feeling of credit, though it is easier to accept.

So here they are and they want to advance in our society economically. One of the traditional ways in the past was through home ownership. And since this was a Bank of America sponsored program there was the not too heavily pushed opportunity to apply for a home loan upon completion and having met certain criteria. The most common way to homeownership is through a home loan. Also buying a car frequently involves the borrowing of money to finance the car. And a job, especially in a city may require a car if public transportation is not available for any number of reasons; shift hours outside operating hours or route availability.

So in many instances getting a job almost mandates having a car. This is especially common for immigrants who sometimes can only find jobs at odd hours or in remote locations. You need money to buy a car and you need a job to get money. So there you are caught. Also, in order to rent an apartment requires a credit history which you do not get if you only spend cash.

Then the reverse danger is to fail to understand that credit is not play money, that there is a real value and cost to credit. It is a complicated situation. So part of my job was to make the concept of credit clear, accurate, and understandable. I used to advise in the beginning that a healthy way to think of credit was to consider which will last longer the bill or the item. Not a perfect solution but workable for what could be considered credit infants.

That's just one example of what we bring to our decision making or even daily living. Knowledge is a type of power, and it is a type of power we can acquire and exercise as well as accumulate.

The kind of knowledge we bring to our decisions, and our actions will affect the sorts of things we do. Yet our knowledge can both become a tool for our happiness or a weapon for our suffering. We can impact our environment and affect our environmental causes in both positive and negative ways. Thus either compounding our happiness or suffering.

What do you bring to your decisions? Are you able to seek out assistance and know when to do so and where to do so when you just don't have all the skills you need? This is important. To have the power and the nature to realize you have neither the power or nature to solve your problem.

Twisted Up / Worn Down: Nyoze Riki

We think sometimes we have unlimited energy, or capacity to keep on going. Sometimes we need this kind of thinking as it enables us to plow on through some tough obstacles. There is the potential though of engaging in this pursuit of endless energy and use it as a default way of living.

It is possible to do this, I suppose, though more likely it is only possible to do this effectively for a short period of time without some negative consequences. We are not wells of infinite energy and capacity. At least we are not without some renewal. The well can run dry and then there isn't anymore to call up. What we do manage to squeeze out of that energy well has to come from someplace, and usually it comes at a much greater expense to some other aspect of our lives.

There are two images that come to mind one is that of a coiled spring or a wilting flower. The image I'm using here can be looked at in both ways. Horizontally it is like a coiled or uncoiled spring. If you look at vertically it could be seen as a wilting line.

As we consume more of our energy or capacity to get things done we deplete that within us as I have mentioned. Some consequences of this are stress, which would be natural since our body is trying to tell us we're running low and the needle will soon be on E. Our stressed self is frequently manifest in our nature and also in our appearance as well as a gradually diminishing capacity. If we ignore this long enough it might have long term consequences.

I look at images of Barack Obama, or any president recently who's had a lot of photos taken of them during their time as president. In every case you can see how much they aged in 8 years, or sometimes even fewer. When Mr. Obama came into office his hair was nice and dark. Perhaps there were a few grey flecks but mostly it was dark. You look at the photos of him when he left office or even now and he is completely white headed. The same can be seen on all previous presidents. The demands of the office are unrelenting and I can only imagine the stresses felt.

It's true I've not been a fan of many of the past presidents, or at least not an ardent supporter, and yet in every case I have great respect for the energy they devoted to doing what they felt was in the best interest of the country. I'll withhold comments about our current president Mr. Trump. I'm not sure I'll ever respect him, just as I will not ever forget Nixon's time in office.

Well guess what folks, the same thing happens to us, we age faster when we are stressed and the degree to which we keep stressing will manifest in our appearance. You know the usually suspects, grey hair faster than what might have been normal, increased lines on the face, tightening of muscles in back and shoulders.

An interesting book titled <u>Back In Control: A Surgeon's Road-map Out of Chronic Pain</u> by David Hanscom, MD, talks about this surgeon's shift in his treatment of chronic back pain away from surgery. He details how, now he will not perform surgery on anyone who does not follow his course which includes keeping a detailed journal for six months among other things. Whereas previously in his practice surgery was the first go to solution, now it is journaling. Through this process he has helped people see how the stresses of their lives, the lifestyle they have engaged in are more often than not the culprit of their pain. He admits it's a tough sell at first because no one wants to admit it and surgery sounds like such a quick fix so why not do it, since life is mostly about quick fixes right.

Over the course of treatment beginning with the journaling he leads his patients in a program that has proven to be more effective than surgery. In fact it was because he was performing surgeries and still people continued to have back problems that led him to reevaluate his approach. I highly recommend this book to anyone who has back problems and especially before considering surgery. The work of this surgeon is merely one example of how interconnected our physical body is to our spiritual/ emotional/mental self.

What goes on in one of the Ten Aspects manifests in all the others equally and connectedly. Think about how debilitating any pain is. If you've had any type of back pain either short term or long term you will know that it seriously limits all of your other activities, your mental state, your everything. Pain also has a cascading effect due to decreased mobility the very thing that can help to alleviate the pain as well as keep the rest of the body in shape.

While I'm on the subject of pain and how it limits us beyond the physical sensation if your really curious about pain then you will find that the increase amount of research into pain, what it is, what it does, and how to manage it is encouraging. Science, and medical science has come a long way into pain research within a span of only a few years. Pain is an interesting and complex phenomena and often times our understanding and treatment of pain has worked at cross purposes.

Working in the hospital enabled me to see how detrimental inactivity can be. A day in bed for a senior can mean a loss in mobility and muscular conditioning that can take weeks if not months to recover from. There is an increased effort now in hospitals to keep patients out of their beds while they are admitted to treatment whenever possible. It just gets worse the less we do. And conversely it gets worse if we try to do too much.

The middle way is certainly the Golden Way. This is where the Eightfold Path interplays with the Ten Suchnesses. There really isn't anything in Buddhism that can be taken completely out of context with other aspects of Buddhism.

When you reach that point of diminishing capacity more than likely it can cause frustration. Here I'll draw from my own life. As I've aged I am no longer able to get up and go like I did when I was younger. There are many things that have changed, mobility, energy, strength, vision, and so on. At times when I forget these things I over-do it and then suddenly I'm caught short. Not only am I caught short I get frustrated that I can't do what I wanted to do or do it the way I used to.

When I travel now I have gotten in the habit of not thinking I can walk everywhere with suitcase in tow. I always budget for taxis and have no problem now spending the extra money to take a cab so that I can arrive at my destination not completely exhausted or even worse, falling down. This last trip to Japan Myokei and I took cabs practically everywhere especially if we had our suitcases. The energy and effort of navigating stations with luggage added to the distances needed to walk with said luggage is too depleting and so we decided we weren't going to be depleted, at least not hauling luggage.

At Mount Minobu the hills are steep and everywhere you walk you will at some point on the journey need to walk up those steep inclines. Going down to the village means walking back up to the lodging temple. Walking up to Kuon-ji means thankfully the return trip is downhill. Last year my breathing condition was so bad I could not go anywhere, it was both disappointing and frustrating. I wasn't able to get up to Kuon-ji for morning service and I wasn't able to get down to the village to say hello to various shop keeper I know or to have ice cream.

This year, with new medication, I was able to do all the walking I wanted. Admittedly I would need to stop frequently along the way to catch my breath and rest my legs and knees but through carefully monitoring my body I was able to walk with wisdom and skill. True not as fast as ten years ago yet not as immobile as the previous year. All in all I'll take it gladly.

Stress also affects our nature as it can cause us to lash out inappropriately. This was certainly the case on the trip to Belgium and then to France immediately afterwards which

Myokei and I made together in 2017. By the end of the trip Myokei and I both were so tired and so stressed that we struggled at times communicating with each other the last two days. We both realized that we needed to pay closer attention to our own self-care, time outs were beneficial.

I recall the time my partner, Wayne, and I were driving across country in 1976. We had shipped our car from Hawaii to San Francisco. The journey to Rhode Island held many unexpected events for us. One was nearly freezing to death twice. The car, being an older one and prior to Hawaii requiring heaters in all cars had no heater. Our plan was to stop at a junk yard in Utah and get one from another car. Well let me tell you driving through the desert in October it gets mighty cold at night. We had to keep stopping every few miles to find a place to warm up, we still had no winter clothes.

Then after we got the heater and continued on our way through Colorado we got caught in an unexpected early blizzard. The car began to stall out and finally on a dark and snowy covered section in the middle of nowhere the car died and wouldn't go any further. We were fortunate that the first vehicle that passed us used in CB radio, yep that's the means of communication before cell phones, to radio to any person behind him that there were stranded motorists on the side of the road. The very next truck that came along had begun to slow down so he could pick us up and give us a lift. He then took us to a ski resort and the local gas station there.

The guys in the station took us to a lodge, which had not opened for the season yet, woke up the keeper who then prepared a room and bed for us and hot chocolate. The guys at the gas station assured us they would go pick up the car and we could come back in the morning. Well for no charge at the inn and only $25 for the car we found out that the gas line had frozen due to the accumulation of water probably from its time in Hawaii and such things were simply not thought about.

In our years together I did most of the driving, and that was the case as we entered into New York City. I'll tell you I have never been so afraid in my life. All I could think about was the car dying on us again and being stranded on a NY freeway and then dying because no one would care. We would simply shrivel up, die, and decompose and no one would mind. Then the traffic, I'd never seen any traffic like NY before in my life. Finally as we were about to cross one of the many bridges I freaked out. I had a death grip on the steering wheel, my knuckles were white and my arms were shaking. All of a sudden I burst out in tears crying and screaming in fright. Wayne didn't know what to think of that, something neither of us had ever done or experienced before. Finally we pulled over and switched driving. I could immediately feel the fear and stress drain from me.

We made it to Rhode Island and spent the winter there. It was my first experience of snow and I became hooked. Now I get to live in a place where it snows a lot, frequently, and reliably. I am so lucky.

The freaking out, while it was a manifestation of my stress, also impacted my environment, and Wayne, my partner. He began to freak out because he didn't understand what was happening, I didn't understand what was happening nor why he was reacting the way he was. It was a ball of stretched rubber bands about to explode. Fortunately we managed to unwind it, and the best we came up with at the time was on our eventual trip to Virginia at the end of his brief tour in Rhode Island I would not be driving the leg through New York. It worked out well. I still have this fear of New York.

As important as it is to know when you are depleting or depleted it is equally important to know what it takes to restore and replenish your capacity, your ability, your power. Often times it may not be what you think. For example, generally, watching TV or surfing the internet or spending time on social media are not power regenerative activities. They may be numbing or lulling but rarely do they provide the kind of nourishment our spirits need. There is compelling evidence that they may in fact exacerbate certain stresses, anxiety, insomnia, diminishing human connections and deep conversations.

How well do you really know yourself and how able are you to listen to your whole body, your deep spirit and your deep physicality? As we are surrounded more and more by things that stimulate us from outside ourselves we are frequently loosing the ability to listen to ourselves. Silence is good example. Many people avoid silence as if it were a menace. I've heard people say I get restless when it's silent so to them it means silence is a bad thing because they associate it with their restlessness. The fact of the mater is they are in fact to some degree experiencing a withdrawal from stimulation and their body doesn't know how to deal with that.

Silence is about the best restorative available. Some other beneficial restorative, rejuvenating activities are hobbies such as painting, knitting, sewing, gardening, walking, hiking, boating, sitting outside in nature even if only on a patio or deck. It is the things we can do or already do that don't require us to think, so to speak. They are often repetitive and some might say they are mind numbing.

This may sound counterintuitive for a Buddhist who latches onto only one meaning of mindfulness. Sometimes mindfulness is not thinking about anything at all and just letting the mind wander where it will. Being non-productive can be very restorative. The trick is to move beyond the withdrawal from stimulation, not always easy.

I know someone who spent some time in a care facility where no TV, radio, internet, or cell phones were allowed. After a while they wrote a letter to me saying how peaceful it was in the morning to listen to the birds chirping as they began their day. You see, we miss that when we immediately turn on the TV, radio, or internet which drowns out the noises of our environment. It's true some environments are indeed a cacophony of noises not directly related to nature. Yet even sitting with that noise, the horns honking, the tires on pavement, the sirens of emergency vehicles, even the neighbors talking is all part of who we are and where we are. Sitting with it for a few moments before we inundate ourselves with manufactured stimulation can be quite peaceful if you let yourself be at peace.

Your nature may need some adjustment around this and that might be something you realize you've not attended to so much in the past.

Scattered / Undecided: Nyoze Sa

Decisions, decisions, decisions.

Life is rife with decisions to be made.

I'm currently reading through the many books written by Terry Pratchett, quite enjoyable and very much a poke in the eye of life, society, government, and human relations.

An interesting belief found commonly among the wizards of the Unseen University and witches as well as even some among the City Guard, is that life is like a pair of trousers. You make a decision and you go down one leg of the trouser while at the same time another or alternate you goes down the other leg of the trousers. A variation on this is the idea that there are in existence an infinite number of you living out an infinite number of paths and choices made. Expanding on this is the notion that any decision you make is the right one and never fear any alternate choices you did not make are being played out someplace. Consequently it really doesn't matter what your choice is what matters it you do something.

Sometimes the choices we have are not always ideal. There may be times when our choice needs to be made between two or more bad options. It can't be helped. The causes we have made previously are now manifesting as a limited

range of poor options. This is not the fault of something outside ourselves though we may wish to believe otherwise and even may act otherwise.

All life is a never ending series of actions to be carried out. Breathing is an action of our lungs inhaling and then exhaling. There is a belief the out-breath is the breath of death. It is the last breathing action our bodies will perform. The out-breath is the breath that is guaranteed. The lungs will collapse upon death and the air inside will be exhaled. The in-breath is the breath of life, it is only because we are alive that we are able to take an in-breath. The next in-breath is not promised to us, however your next out breath is certain.

Breathing is just one of my actions we engage in every moment of our lives. Some of the actions happen automatically or without any conscious mental effort. Other actions may require us to consider the doing. What will I have for dinner, what clothes shall I wear, shall I go shopping or instead stay home and read a book? These and countless other decisions are ones we make throughout a day, a week, a month, a year, a lifetime. We make some of the decisions over and over again endlessly.

When I was in the 11th grade our family didn't have much money. I was working part-time while going to high school and the little money I made I was trying to save for college. That year because of those economic factors I only had two shirts to wear. Yes I probably could have spared the money to buy a couple more, yet it seemed like a frivolous expense. And so I would wear the same shirt every other day, both of them were madras shirts and so they actually almost looked identical. Of course I hoped no one would notice that I was wearing the same shirts every day.

They did notice and most people said nothing. A couple of folks commented and asked why I was wearing the same shirts all the time. I felt slightly embarrassed even as I explained I didn't have money for any more shirts. Strangely the end result was my standing in school grew and more people began to like me. I was asked to join a secret high school fraternity, one only the 'special kids' belonged to. It was kind of unsettling in that all the things you would think you need to do to be cool, didn't really need to be done. You just needed to be as authentic and real as you possibly can. Crazy huh?

Why did I bring this up here, you may wonder. Well, our activities are in fact impacted by our power and ability to carry out certain activities. My resources were limited and so the options for various actions were limited. That in turn affected the causes I was making, even causes I wasn't aware I was making. Further more those actions impacted my environment.

Now, maybe it wasn't just the two shirts, maybe it was my nature, my honesty, my embarrassment, maybe folks just felt sorry for me. And I know the story doesn't always end favorably, not for everyone. There are after all a myriad of possibilities, and infinite number of universes, two legs to a trouser.

Regardless, our decisions, and our actions are all impacted by our power to carry out those decisions and actions. This in turn will have an effect on our causes and our environment.

Our power can be limited in any number of ways, and often due to the nature of the thing requiring our action. Sometimes our will power is not sufficient to carry out the actions we know would be in our best interest. It is times like this when our congruence is not aligned. This is an invitation to us, though we may not wish to accept it, to examine what is causing the disconnect.

It might be that our thoughts about what we should do or what would be the best action is more shallow than we suspect. Perhaps, and often most likely the case is we have only a superficial desire to do the best thing. That is a rather harsh personal assessment, because we want to think we are good people always acting in perfect accord with our best intentions to achieve an optimal life with minimal suffering. Perhaps a person my then lean to thinking they are weak-willed.

I wouldn't put such a label on it as being weak-willed. I think it might be more like not-fully-willed, or partially-willed. While one part of our mind knows fully well what would be the best course of action, another part hasn't quite made the same commitment. So not all the parts of yourself, your mind are in full accord or agreement with each other.

Primary Cause: Nyoze In

This morning, Tuesday, 7 August 2018, I was walking my dog shortly after sunrise and besides enjoying the unscripted walk, the sunny sky, I was thinking about this Aspect of Primary Cause. I had been trying to come up with some examples to help illustrate the concept of a primary cause versus any other cause we may make.

Two ideas came to my mind and I immediately told my dog to sit, which she did and she is always patient with me when I do that in the middle of the walk. It's as if she knows something needs to be done and all that is required of her is to wait. I always carry my notebook and my phone yet it's always the notebook I turn to. The phone is with me for photos and emergencies.

The notebook is my go to resource for recording ideas. I immediately jotted them down with a short explanation. Then freeing those thoughts from my mind and giving myself the assurance they would not be forgotten I was able to think of them a bit more. It's a great process, freeing up your mind so you don't have to think about forgetting something, in fact you can actually forget it safely with it written down.

The way I look at Primary Cause is it's the cause before the other causes except it's not always the first cause. This is where I think a couple of illustrations may be helpful.

In my printmaking art the process usually begins with an idea and drawing. That may on the surface seem like a primary cause yet I don't consider it to be such. Let me go on. So I've got my idea, drawn my image now I have currently four options for making the print and each one will yield a completely different print even if the image is identical.

I now make a choice between carving the image on linoleum, rubber, or sheet PVC, or I could choose to do an etching. Each one of those will yield a different representation of the image. The etching would be the most dramatically different. Of the three substrates to carve each one, linoleum, rubber, PVC carve differently, yield edges and lines differently, circles and curves are different for each one. The linoleum generally will allow for the most fine details, the rubber does circles and curves easier yet the lines are softer, the PVC doesn't do well with fine details. The PVC and rubber have a much longer life span for printing where as the linoleum will only last in its best condition for about 10 years.

The choice I make at this point I consider to be the Primary Cause. From the point of selecting the carving medium every other cause that is directed to the completion of the art will be tied to the substrate I use to carve. The image didn't necessarily limit my choices, though it can sometimes. The image was merely the seed for the Primary Cause. The medium though will impact every other aspect of the image, the printing, the final outcome, it is all tied to the type of block I choose.

While the art image initially as the first cause for the project is not the Primary Cause for the finished art. Primary here does not mean first or initial, it means the cause that all the other subsequent causes are impacted by.

Another example directly related to Buddhism is the myth behind Seigaki, or Feeding the Hungry Ghosts. In the myth Maudgalyayana, Mokuren in Japanese, goes searching for his deceased mother using his supernatural powers in the various realms of the dead. Initially he searched in vain in all the heavenly realms, and finally was shocked to find his mother in the Realm of Hungry Ghosts.

What was so shocking about his mother being in one of the hell realms was that she was a great supporter of the Buddha making very large generous financial offerings to the Sangha. Yet her outward generosity masked her desire for fame. In other words she gave so she could look like a devotee, she gave to look good.

In this case the Primary Cause was not the donations it was her attitude that lay underneath the donations. Every cause that stemmed from that Primary Cause of appearing to be devote or to look good was impacted and affected by that Primary Cause.

I won't leave you hanging here, and I won't assume all those who read this know the whole story so I'll finish telling you about how we come to celebrate Seigaki.

As I mentioned Maudgalyayana, found his mother suffering in the Realm or Hell of Hungry Ghosts. In his sympathy for his mother he tried to provide her water and nourishment. Yet every attempt to do so only caused his mother more anguish. The water boiled and burned her the food would burst into flames. Maudgalyayana was so distraught he went to the Buddha to find out why his mother was in such a hell and how he could alleviate her suffering.

The Buddha told him that while his mother was very generous on the surface her generosity was actually a greedy act. She was greedy for recognition and praise for her donations. Generosity was greed for her. The Buddha said the only way to provide any relief or nourishment was to offer the Sutra, or by some versions make offering to all the monks, on the 15th day of the seventh month.

In Nichiren Shu we offer the Lotus Sutra as well as various sweets, candies, other delicacies. Some Sanghas make this almost like Halloween, a Buddhist Halloween if you will. While the 15th day of the seventh month was prescribed it was based on the lunar calendar and so the date can and is somewhat fungible. The idea for the date was based upon the completion of the annual summer retreat observed during the time of the Buddha. So, why not on October 31st?

The Primary Cause impacts all causes. If our primary cause is a fundamental belief, even if unidentified or unknown, for our own benefit then the subsequent causes are affect by that Primary Cause. There can be and are numerous Primary Causes. A lie begets another lie. A structure built on a poor foundation no matter how elegant is not a sound structure and certainly will collapse. The Primary Cause while not necessarily the first cause is the cause which binds all the causes and influences them, either for good or for ill.

Environmental Cause: Nyoze En

Having a perfect day, nothing going wrong, and nothing foreseeable to go wrong, you joyfully live your life. Bam, all of a sudden something happens and everything changes. In a heartbeat or the blink of an eye your life is turned upside down and inside out or worse.

You have now been hit by an environmental cause, that is something that arises outside of your direct action. This could be a rain shower, car accident, stock market news, earthquake, canceled air flight, flat tire, crowded bus, and so on the list could go to infinity. It happens to us all and it happens all the time without interruption.

There are two ways of considering Environmental Causes, yet there is really only one way - two ways but one way.

Of the two ways they are it's not your fault and it's your fault. Really though it is all of your doing. The complication and the important thing to remember is you have made the cause at some time to be in the situation to experience the current environmental cause and you have no way to undo or affect it now. So in a way while it is your cause in the past and there is nothing now to do except experience it and make new causes.

Another consideration of Environmental cause is like planting a garden. The place were you live, the environmental weather conditions are beyond your control, except you decided to live there. Well, perhaps you didn't actually have a free hand at the decision, it could have been the only alternative for your job, and yet that too is of your doing. You see there is quite a rabbit hole there to pursue, not exactly pointless, yet must be navigated wisely if navigating is desired.

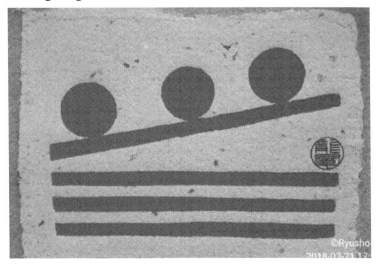

It can be a lesson in the interconnectedness of our causes from past to present and learning from that can be beneficial. One must remember though that those past causes are unchangeable and so the lessons gained can only be applied to present circumstances; how not to make the same mistakes again.

So you've decided to plant a garden, and let's say you live in a snowy region such as Syracuse were I live. I have fond memories of bougainvillea plants from my time in Hawaii and San Diego, they are prolific bloomers and the color range is quite large. So I decide that on thing I want for sure is one of them in my garden growing up a trellis in the back.

Sorry, that's going to fail.

The fact of the matter is no matter how much care I give the plant this is an environment where it will not grow outdoors. It gets too cold and doesn't get hot enough.

The crepe myrtle only grows in the United States below the Mason Dixon Line, above that line it's too cold a climate. When I lived in Charlotte crepe myrtle grow prolifically and I always swore that the next place I lived would be a place where crepe myrtle can not grow. It was a measure for me of a place to warm to live if it was warm enough for the crepe myrtle.

The environment impacts us both as an effect and as a cause. The environment, and this is not only weather, it is culture, activities, any outside stimulus on our lives is an environment. A sports game is an environment, an airplane is an environment. Those environments both act upon us and also limit us and the causes we can make. They are directly tied to us and also tie us.

While you are in this moment having a perfect day something in your environment can and does impact that experience it also determines to a degree the range of options for further causes either by you or by the environment. No mater how much power you have as an entity that power will be impacted by and impacted upon by the environment you are existing in.

While it is true the environment impacts upon us and our ability to make certain causes we still have agency in that environment within reason. Just because everyone around you is angry at the clerk in Walmart doesn't mean you to need to add to that environment of anger. You don't need to add more energy there. But you may not be physically endowed enough to tell everyone to be quiet, so your entity is going to limit your range of possible actions, your mood will also be a consideration in your actions, and so on. Do you see how this is all tied together.

To speak of environmental causes as a separate aspect without considering how it relates to all the other aspects will lead to a misunderstanding and unskillful actions.

It is true that we could stop everything and regard all options logically, pulling a Spock or Data if you will. But the reality is life moves incredibly fast and for most of us we are acting in an auto pilot mode. Here is where a daily practice is so important.

When we gradually hone our live with the Odaimoku, we slowly chip away at the unskillful patterns logged deeply in our life that would automatically emerge in stressful situations or situations where there is only time to act and not time to think. Slowly the default mode of operation can become Buddha, and that influences all the aspects of our lives just as Hell can impact them.

Effects: Nyoze Ka

One challenge when studying Buddhism is to not go down the normal human path of analyzing every thing as independent theories. While for the sake of explaining the various theories we find in Buddhism does require us to break things down it does have the potential of misleading us into thinking of everything as being separated. We can study Ten World and do so without examining any other related theory, yet this only provides a limited and misleading understanding. Granted it is simpler to do things in small chunks yet by doing so we can miss the larger truth revealed by the chunks in whole.

The Ten Aspects is one part of the theory of Ichinen Sanzen, or what is commonly called Three Thousand Conditions of Mind in a Single Moment. That's quite a lot of theory contained in the Japanese terms. To get to this number we combine the Ten Worlds, Ten Aspects, and Three Factors. This book is my attempt to explain the Ten Aspects, a subset of the 3000 that often gets less publicity than the Ten Worlds.

The Ten Worlds are easily broken down into ten individual categories or realms or conditions of life/mind. The Ten Worlds as we are taught each contain the Ten Worlds within each world. So we could theoretically say there is a Hell/Hell world, a Hell/Hunger world, Hell/Animality world, Hell/Anger world, Hell/Human world, Hell/Heaven world, Hell/Self-taught world, Hell/Learning world, Hell/ Bodhisattva world, Hell/Buddha world. And then we can do it all over again with Hunger/Hell, Hunger/Hunger and so on until we have done this one hundred times going through each of the possible combinations of ten within ten.

At the end of this process I personally have to wonder what have we accomplished other that will enable us to end our suffering and enable us to attain enlightenment? Not everyone is like me so there may indeed be some who find this sort of abstraction beneficial. I find it more of a distraction and since I'm writing the book and I really can only write from my point of view that's what I'm going to do.

When I teach Ten Worlds theory I prefer teaching it not as theory of trying to figure out which box we are currently in at the moment. Rather it think it more valuable to think of the Ten Worlds as a map to hep us navigate from wherever we are in this moment to where we would like to go.

One advantage to approaching the Ten Worlds from this perspective is we don't need to really know where we are. It helps of course to know in what realm or state of mind you are in, but it really isn't as fundamentally important as knowing where you want to be.

Let's say you are really in deep suffering, so deep that it certainly feels like hell, yet it could be hunger or anger, and they can be confused easily enough. That is perhaps the single most valuable part of realizing that each of the Ten Worlds contain all the other Ten Worlds. Well that and knowing that even in your deepest darkest state of suffering there is always Buddha. And too, even in your best most angelic self there is also hell.

Thinking of the Ten Worlds as a map allows us to look at the kind of life or the conditions of mind that are manifest in the realm we aspire to. For example we say we want to become Buddhas and be enlightened, yet how well do we know what that sort of life looks like.

Now I've been with people in the hospital who are in such a state of suffering that is so low they can't even imagine looking as high as enlightenment. In a way the crowd seated on the ground when the Buddha went up into the treasure tower and sat beside Many Treasures Buddha were like that. They entreated the Buddha to raise them up so they could at least see the Buddha.

While this isn't a perfect example, sometimes we need to first be raised up a little just so we can see a little light reflecting off Enlightenment. One of the easiest first destinations on the Ten Worlds road map to Enlightenment is Humanity. That is a realm that is the first stop out of the lower realms of suffering. It is the first realm populated by humans, which is what we are. In a way our dwelling in the lower realms is living with denizens, animals, and fearsome non-human entities. We as humans really don't belong there but we can get trapped or seduced into them and then we suffer.

Another reason why striving for the realm of Humanity if we are in the deepest of the suffering realms is illustrated best if we understand the Ten Aspects.

As I've mentioned previously the Ten Aspects are not so easily nor effectively understood as separate things. They are not intended to be considered separately independent from each other. The Ten Aspects all look different depending upon the World we are inhabiting at any moment.

In any of the lower realms all of the physical parts of the Ten Aspects, Appearance, Entity, Nature, Power and so forth are weak, and greatly diminished and this is also a contributing factor to remaining in a cycle of suffering in the Four Lower Worlds.

Because a person in Hell lacks the nature of understanding the reality of suffering and how suffering begets suffering, they repeat the causes of their suffering. While there may be and often is a lot of energy which we may consider power we find people in Hell lashing out as it were to their environment. Anger often arises easily and Anger has its own Power, it's destructive. The Primary Cause of Anger is Power if you will. Think of Asura the speck of a demon who when enraged blows itself up into their fearsome demon. The Angry person is not meek before the subject of its anger. When was the last time you saw an Angry person shrink before the person they are angry with?

Anger's Primary Cause, its Power, it Nature and so forth all contribute to the conditions which will ensure its continued suffering. Anger is frequently borne of arrogance and we see that in Asura. An arrogant person is either fearful of someone better or always discontent with the inferiority of others. Anger shows on a person's face, it reveals itself in every muscle of a person body.

The lower realms are like this which is why they become a cycle of suffering. The things that cause anger are repeated.

A person suffers, they lash out at their environment and the weakest things they can find frequently are other people or animals. They are powerless, or think they are to change their environment and so they act in unskillful ways. They do not see that the path to ending suffering is through Humanity and the shared human experience of feelings, compassion, connection. The human Activities and Primary Causes are the first and easiest steps to alleviating suffering available.

They say that, and I do believe it to be so, petting a dog can lower one's blood pressure and heart rate, can reduce stress, and bring a sense of calmness to one's being. Petting a dog is the action of connection, of realizing that we are not alone in the world, we are not alone in experiencing pain, we are not alone in frustrations and so forth.

Hunger, is greed, it is self-directed and all the Aspects of self will reinforce this and increase the suffering. What is needed is to begin to exert our power, however limited we may think it is by making causes to become human.

Understanding the map of the Ten Worlds and realizing that the Ten Aspects are how we live or manifest the Ten Worlds gives us the tools or key to ending our suffering.

Rewards and Retributions: Nyoze Ho

Frequently it is necessary to remind ourselves that in Buddhism there is no punishment for not doing your practice. In the ten aspects we read rewards and retribution and it would be an easy mistake to think there is punishment in Buddhism.

The fact is this phrase only refers to how we might consider the effects of our causes, the primary cause and the environmental cause. If there is no cause made then there is a consequent absence of effect. So if you skip your practice there is simply an absence of a cause, not the creation of a bad cause. That would fly in the face of the laws of cause and effect. You simply can not get a bad effect from no cause.

Now as to the nature of reward and retribution. The impact of the effects you experience from the causes you make are in fact the result of a cause you make. If you perceive something as wholly bad or negative that is ultimately your cause, or the cause you are making as a result of the effect you experience.

Every effect is an opportunity to make further causes. This where karma comes in, or the proper understanding of karma. Your nature, or your tendency to respond to the effects you experience sets the stage for you to continue to experience effects of similar types. For example if you are by nature currently an high anger type person then it is more likely that you will see an opportunity to become angry in most of the effects that happen in your life. It will be easier for you to become angry than it will for you to see good or value in effects of your life.

So because your nature tends to anger, your causes also tend to anger and generate the kinds of causes that will tend to repeat the cycle. It isn't so much that your karma is to be angry, rather it is your karma to act angry and generate effects matching your causes.

Whether an effect is a reward or retribution depends solely upon you. If say something that we would consider bad happens to you, what is critical is what you do as a result of that effect. If you continue to make causes similar to the ones that resulted in this present effect then you could conceivably say they are retributions. If however you say, man that sucked I don't want that to happen again, and then examined what caused it and determine not to repeat that cause then even a seemingly bad effect becomes a reward.

The reward is the lesson to not repeat a cause that harms you or inclines you to hate, or anger, or suffering. And sometimes what can seem to be a reward is actually a retribution. This is especially the case if we become complacent in happiness or good fortune and fail to continue to make appropriate causes to ensure those things continue. Then even good fortune becomes bad.

This is not simply the power of positive thinking or happy-go-lucky. No, this is about deeply considering one's situation and one's participation in life. Not having money to buy food sucks, and this isn't about somehow contriving a way to put a positive spin on an empty stomach. Rather it is an invitation, if you will, to consider the situation as painful and something worthy of changing if possible. An empty stomach hurts regardless what religion you practice, and Buddhism doesn't automatically make air into food.

Buddhism is about examining our experiences and seeking to understand why they are that way, what can be done to either mitigate or change or eliminate the effects by making new causes. There isn't some magic that takes place which replaces the necessity of making new causes. Buddhism is not a short cut to wealth, fame, ease, and luxury. Buddhism is a religion of hard work, honest evaluation of one's life, sincere effort to make necessary changes, and the dedication to carry out these for the duration of one's life continually.

The reward or retribution depends not on just how you view a circumstance, it is about what you do with that circumstance. First you are a human-being, and then you must be a human-doing.

Equality: Nyoze Honmatsu Ku Kyo To

Every day for as long as we live if we are lucky we engage in various activities. Eating, sleeping, personal hygiene, are a few of the basics which occupy our time and attention. Depending upon our age we these basics will be performed differently and will probably look different. If we are old such as myself, hygiene includes trimming hairs from my ears, an activity I did not need to do when I was in my 20s and 30s, and one I wish I still did not need to do. Shaving is another thing that has been different over my life. When I was younger, because my hair grew slowly and sparsely I only needed to shave twice a week. As I got older into my 40s it changed and I needed to shave every day. Now that I'm retired I'm back to shaving about twice a week, because no one cares if I have a stubble.

Work activities are also changing as we age or even as we change jobs. During our younger and middle years we may find our jobs, as a means for providing income, occupies great chunks of our time daily, weekly, and monthly. As we get older that intensity of work may decline even if the physical actions might become more difficult and strenuous due to changes in our bodies.

Eating habits change over lifetimes, perhaps for the better or perhaps not. Reading likes and dislikes may change. Physical ability certainly changes and not always simply because of aging, perhaps an injury caused a permanent change. Every thing in our lives is subject to change. This is of course a Buddhist belief that there is no thing which remains unchanged forever, including ourselves.

So while all of those thing are changing the needs of nourishment to our spirit, our well being, or our wholeness also changes. The notion of self-care, which is experiencing a growing awareness, is vital to our continued well being, our sanity even. Subtle changes occur to our personality, our responses to environmental changes, our relationships to name a few are all connected to how well we take care of our self.

Self-care is often confused with or thought of as being selfish. It is sometimes thought that if I take care of myself then I am not taking care of someone else. And that someone else may be a spouse, a child, a sick family member or friend. Yet self-care is not being selfish.

In my work as a chaplain I would remind folks that what happens to the person you are caring for if you become sick or unable to do the things you do? In fact those we may care for require us to take care of ourselves also.

It's not always about taking care of someone sick though. In relationships such as marriage or raising children the other person may not be sick, they may be perfectly healthy yet you are part of a team so to speak and that team requires you to be whole and healthy for it to function in a normal healthy fashion. If you are inattentive to a spouse then that sows the seeds for discontent, and if it's a child then there may be behavioral issues. There may, depending upon the degree that one's self is not whole, be trauma done to the situation.

Here is where balance is important. There is a fine line, one which each of us needs to find for ourselves between fulfilling all of our many responsibilities outside of our self and the responsibility within one's self. For too much self-care can indeed become selfish, and even too little self-care can be also selfish.

The Eightfold Path in Buddhism offers us many ways of examining our lives through the lens of skillfulness. Developing the capacity to see into the actions and the outcomes seeking to walk the line between doing good and avoiding harm. The degree we are able to, with skill, walk the middle path between harm and good has a direct impact on our physical being as well as our spiritual and psychological or mental well being.

Balance is about doing the least harm while accomplishing the greatest good.

The phrase nyoze honmatsu ku kyo to translates to their equality as such despite these differences. In other words, all of our being, the physical and the non-physical aspects, all are affected by one another. When one area of our self is out of whack then so too will be the other aspects. While we may not at first perceive the manifestation in things such as our appearance, nature, or entity we certainly can notice that our energy declines as we become tired. Tiredness is only one manifestation, others are more subtle.

When I was deeply immersed in the caring of young boys dying from AIDS it seemed as if it would never end. One after another these young men were dying and there was nothing I could do to stop it from happening. Yet not doing something was not an option for me. As the number of guys dying grew an the amount of effort I put in became greater and greater I began to change.

The changes were subtle and in fact it wasn't until some time later that I was aware they had occurred. Unbeknownst to me my temper began to become shorter, I would anger quickly, and my frustration grew. That frustration had to be released because we each have a limit to how much frustration we can hold. We each have a limit to how much grief we can ignore, or how much pain we can suppress. The limit is different for each of us yet the limit is there.

The total grief, frustration, and anger accumulated inside and it sought ways of escaping. Because I was not aware of this and because I did not adequately take care of my self, mending my spirit the consequences manifest in my expression of anger towards others and situations I experienced. It wasn't until I moved from San Diego to Charlotte and stepped out of the caring for the dying environment that I began to realize that I had indeed changed from not taking care of myself.

I spent a couple of years not working with folks with HIV/ AIDS and during that time I attended to mending myself. At first I really didn't realize what it was I was doing. I had truly been affected by care-giver fatigue. While a part of me knew this even at the time, there was a part that said I couldn't or shouldn't feel that way, or that it was being selfish to think of my own care when the needs of those dying were so great.

When I did once again connect with a group in Charlotte that was caring for HIV/AIDS patients and families I noticed that my energy for doing the work had changed and that I actually had more energy and that towards the end of the time in San Diego I had become not just emotionally exhausted I had become physically exhausted.

I hope this doesn't sound too convoluted or confusing. Remember I am recounting an experience that I didn't become aware of until after it happened. While it was happening I was oblivious to the subtle changes both in my nature and in my energy yet the changes were occurring.

The fact that something within us changes and we are not aware of it is doubly harmful because in our ignorance we may try to change things or do things that will have a negative impact and not accomplish our goals. My anger at that time did not help to resolve what was going on in my emotions, in fact it only compounded the problem.

This I believe is one of the great advantages of Buddhism. Through the study and practice of our faith we can delve into our self deeply and see the root of our suffering and with the tools provided to us from our faith we can then begin to work on solving the problems of our lives in constructive and beneficial ways.

Conclusion: Why We Recite the Junnyoze Three Times

During our service and the recitation of portions from the Lotus Sutra we recite the Junnyoze from Chapter II three times. You may wonder why that is since it is only written one time in the sutra. I'm surprised more people don't ask about that since it is so clearly at odds with any other recitation we do, repeating something that isn't written.

I suppose it is because some may think they would appear to be asking a dumb question as if they should know it by osmosis. Let me just say that before I began this more in-depth exploration of the Ten Suchnesses I would not have been able to answer it. I was reminded of it by Sensei Ryuei McCormick and his in-depth study of all things Nichiren. I do recall studying it years ago and then I forgot the reason. Since no one asked me I continued to forget.

This is a good lesson on why it's important to ask questions, it keeps people like myself honest. Don't ever think that your question is silly, superfluous, unimportant, or heaven forbid dumb. Working on this I had to ask the question myself.

The fact of our reciting it three times is unique to Nichiren Buddhism and Chih-I. In brief it is the Threefold Contemplation in a Single Mind. There is the Three

Thousand States of Mind and then there is the Three Contemplations of a Single Mind.

Each recitation of the Ten Aspects or Ten Suchnesses is done from a different perspective even though the wording does not actually change. In fact the wording does change in our minds, though this point is lost if we don't learn it. So mostly people merely recite it three times because everyone else is doing it and after all who wants to be the one who raises their hand and says, "yea, but why."

Other schools according to Nichiren[1] only view the Contemplation from the perspective of a single realm. By doing so they ignore the realms of non-substantiality and temporary existence. According to our schools reading the first read is from the point of non-substantiality and so the meaning is; this appearance is thus, this natures is thus, this entities is thus, and so forth. The second reading is from the perspective of temporary existence and so is read in this way; thus appearance, thus nature, thus entity, and so forth. The third and final reading is from the perspective of the Middle Way and reads like this; appearance is thus, nature is thus, entity is thus, and so forth.

On the first reading, the one from the point of view of non-substantiality we are making ourselves or reminding ourselves that we are The Buddha, the Thus Come One of the reward body. All the Ten worlds are non-substantial as at any one moment they contain each other and can manifest any other. This truth is the truth of the reward

1. The Doctrine of Three Thousand Realms in a Single Moment of Life, Writings of Nichiren Diashonin Vol II, page 82-91

body which we acquire when we read it in this way. The reward here being the manifestation of enlightenment even in the presence of the other Ten Worlds.

The second reading reminds us or recalls to us that all things are temporary or impermanent. This is the benefit of the manifest body. The truth of our impermanence is also the truth of the human being Shakyamuni who is the Eternal Buddha.

The third reading calls us to remember that we are the manifestation of the of the Thus Come One of the Dharma Body. We gain the same benefit of the Dharma Body of the Eternal Buddha, that of emancipation and wisdom of the Dharma Body.

In summary we have the Ten Worlds, each possessing all the Ten Worlds equaling 100 Worlds. This is then multiplied by the Ten Aspects giving us 1000. The 1000 is then multiplied by The Three Buddha Bodies giving a total of 3000 Conditions of Mind in a Single Moment of Existence.

There is much more to this portion of Ichinen Sanzen that can be said and for now I will leave it as it is and hold out the hope that soon I will write another book devoted solely to this final point. It is rich with meaning, importance, and complexity deserving it's own study.

This concludes my writing on the subject of the Ten Aspects or Ten Suchnesses. My original thinking was this would be a small book roughly about 24 pages, or two pages per suchness. It ends as a slightly longer book and hopefully not too boring, or difficult. This was only intended to be an entry level exploration into the subject and I believe I've kept it that way, or I hope I have.

I did not devote a separate chapter to the equality aspect because I feel I have covered it all along in the writing and felt there was nothing more to add without simply being redundant.

Thank you for purchasing this book, for reading it, and for considering the subject in relation to your life and your practice in faith to the Lotus Sutra.

With Gassho,
Ryusho Jeffus, Shonin

Connect with Ryusho Jeffus on-line:

Twitter:
@ryusho @myoshoji

Facebook Myosho-ji Temple Page:
https://www.facebook.com/myoshoji

Facebook Author Page:
https://www.facebook.com/revryusho

Blog:
https://www:ryusho.org/blog
https://www.ryusho.org/art

89993378R10042

Made in the USA
Middletown, DE
19 September 2018